AWAKEN THE IMMORTAL WITHIN

Jason Breshears

An Archaix Book

published by

THE BOOK TREE

San Diego, California

© 2022
Jason Breshears

ISBN 978-1-58509-599-5

cover art
© by Space Wind

Editor & layout
Paul Tice

Published by
The Book Tree
San Diego, California
www.thebooktree.com

We provide fascinating and educational products to help awaken the public to new
ideas and information that would not be available otherwise.
Call 1 (800) 700-8733 for our FREE BOOK TREE CATALOG.

CONTENTS

INTRODUCTION

I offered to write this Introduction because the power of the material demanded it. I've spent years, as the author has, studying and exploring the secrets of the universe and ways for one to achieve the betterment of themselves and mankind in general. The astute reader may notice that the further one goes down the rabbit hole to discover such things, the more that is found within these pages as being powerful fruits that were pulled from those depths.

Due to the fact that I am the author's publisher, some may consider this Introduction to be biased. But again, the material demanded it. Books of this nature, short and to the point, are often the most useful and are seldom found. You are therefore in luck with this one – as long as you approach these teachings *seriously*, and spend time in applying them diligently.

In my years of study, I've found only a few books that have the ability to change one's life. This book shows all the earmarks of being such a treasure. It is true that everyone is different, and this book cannot promise to magically transform you. But as long as one approaches this book seriously and puts some effort into applying its principles, there is a real chance.

So in short, the purpose of this brief Introduction is to implore you to consider, very carefully, the potential you have to transform your life into something more powerful and more meaningful than commonly found within this mundane, worldly, hypnotic form of consciousness that society quietly crams down our throats. Herein lies a chance to awaken the Immortal within.

Paul Tice

Chapter One

FIRST STEPS TO AWAKEN

This book is for those who have searched for the truth all their life. You know it is there, but have not found it yet. It is *your* truth being sought, not THE truth. Only you can find it. I cannot give it to you; I can only provide a path. The rest of you are warned away.

Reality is an evasive witch, sweeping away paradigms with the dust of discovery. When a mortal approaches the hallowed realm of what's real, her substance becomes shadow, an immortal jest – the process of discovery exceeding our ability to fully process what it discovered.

Things are rarely as they appear. Because we think, we believe that we are alive, though some distant inner voice whispers secrets. It is the dead who gather to mourn the living... a funeral attracts a congregation of the lost. Or an ancient doctrine – when angels die they become mortal souls. The meaning of life evades the living because nothing is made alive until it dies. A terrible misunderstanding; a misconception manufactured to deceive. We are carcasses of creativity ever compelled to call upon the One that does not answer. Not yet.

Men fear the unknown, the decay of their prisons, unmindful that they are spirits bound in physical, bodily bondage. Cocooned immortality. The individual human is deity dismembered and deceived; billions of ethereal sparks in a ghostly fire. Such is the essence of material reality – all is a reflection of something else, like the future to the past. We sparks are the Undead, condemned to serve a sentence in a hell we call home, flowing through materiality in a struggle like so many spermatozoon racing to fertilize the bondage of another immortal soul. A definition of tragedy: to be born into a realm of death and to grow into the blame.

Religionist beware, you will find no ally here. In death I walked that path till almost lost in darkness. The Deep has no greater voice than those who claim to come from God. It was from this Abyss I came, starving, that I finally found a truth.

Raised a staunch religionist, washed in blood that never flowed from a God who never walked, I was reborn, a spirit-filled unbeliever, crucified in criticism to observe clearly the stage and all that's hidden behind it. Woe unto the scribes! Line upon line, inventiveness masked as inspiration, words dropped by the whims of copyists as others were added, the far east robbed of its parables as the west lost its stage plays.

The Christian story is a cosmopolitan drama – a sculpture of Greek Platonism, Stoic austerity, Alexandrian learning, Ionian Mysteries and Egyptian wisdom – an old Israelite eschatology altered into Jewish forgeries, a statuesque "gnosis" is this pillared story of the Gospel. A soup made of all the best ingredients.

In my search for the Savior I mistook my feelings for His fidelity. Seeking a cause I found a curse. In stepping off the carefully prepared path I saw its destination clearly – to pierce the Veil and fall into a pit. My religion a lie of Maya, I despaired and found no comfort. In wrath I wandered, separated from the world but with sight far and true. A prison world – the abyssal layers of dungeon realms perfected to confuse and confine a host of eternal spirits.

Us.

Intrepid sojourner, with rule and plumb line I searched the depth and marveled at my catch... lying leviathans of Judaism, deceitful monkeys of Hinduism, a hydra of a hundred denominations each guarding a portal to paradise. But the gates of hell are seminaries. The flocks are fleeced with offering plates while fed the grass of guilt. Teaching of a light they spread darkness, with healing on their tongues they spread plague with their handshakes. While praising a Holy Spirit they mask the doubt within their own. Pastors and preachers, reverends and priests – a new species of devil, illusionists turning horns into halos, myths into money, hell into heaven... thundering the Word of God as if the voice of men could speak it.

Jesus is the drama of a paramount ideal, deification ex post facto, the sum total of many ancient parts. He is what we want, not what we have. What we possess is actually so much more powerful. But for now, woe unto the scribes! In rewriting a stage play they invented redemption.

A definition of religion: spiritual population-control propaganda by nonhuman overseers.

The slow developmental transition of eastern cosmology into the historic religions they became, that eventually morphed into the mysticism of today, is a steady record of mankind's attempts to make some sense of the recognizable unreality of his existence. The revolt against Maya, or man's horrific revelation that he is trapped in a multifaceted web of layered illusions designed to blind him from the interconnectedness of all things, resulted in complex philosophical systems that endeavored to justify why terrible things happened to good people. Or how it could be that the immoral and wicked not only remain unpunished, but prosper as well. A secret: there are no ethical considerations of the wolf when rending the rabbit.

Thus the knowledge of Maya, our prison holosphere, was corrupted by a false conception designed to rationalize these problems: the Karmaic Doctrine. The idea that what goes around comes around satisfied many who saw evidence of its operation in the manifestations of events in the lives of good and bad men. But some were not convinced. The believer in Karma saw only what Maya reflected, their own projections – while the critic invented yet another doctrine to explain why he often saw no evidence whatsoever of Karma at work. The new belief explained why there was so little perceived evidence of Karma, that Karmaic debt builds in one life to be discharged in another – or reincarnation.

The transmigration of souls is yet another desperate attempt of humanity to cope with the unfairness of reality, the bitter pain of loss, the unbending phenomenon of

Murphy's Law, with death. Attempting to make sense of his twisted existence, man invented religion, sin-debt, and Maya thus provided mankind with priests to help him interpret realities that burdened humanity with a need for redemption. The victims now blame themselves for their own spiritual enslavement and physical travails, woes compounded on the religious believer who suffers only because he believes he is meant to suffer.

I commend you for reading this far. In stripping away untruths to see what remains intact, it is first necessary to cull the herd. What is REAL is always kept SECRET. Imagine the difficulty of a single spark within a fire realizing that it is the flame, but trapped in a smaller world that confines it. Because it is the masses that make the holospheric matrix, we find that the flame of truth is for the individual and not the masses. A few individuals can share the truth, but not the many. If you are one of these people, this knowledge is for you. In absorbing what I share, you may become one with a larger whole.

Chapter Two

FOUNDATIONAL KNOWLEDGE

You will become a rogue spirit adrift in a sea of humanity with coordinates to islands others cannot see, a vagabond of another vintage. You shall cope with the truth, though you may not believe it. Not at first. By the act of looking you shall perceive invisible cords that pull and oppress others – forces that now shun you, that regard you as an aberrant malfunction in a system of controlled chaos. Infected with curiosity, they will treat you as diseased – the bonds that earlier bound you will be severed to contain this contagion. Holospheric self-preservation. It passes poisons off as remedies, the healthy, few in number. You shall become a medicine man with antidotes in the dark, carrying a torch bearing sacred fire lit by another. In the shadows of this flickering light are enemies encircled; they rage against revelations. Conspirators striving to darken the illumined.

In searching, your gaze will reflect back upon yourself and a truth will be unveiled. A new scion to what lies hidden in the human race. The living emerge only after the egg is cracked... the womb torn. You will remember the future as you see clearly the past. Unto you, the reader, are secrets rendered, obscurities unobstructed. There is truth in what is written – "To him who hath, more will be given..." From opposing vantage points lucidity and lunacy are one: the visionary knowing the holosphere for what it is, while the vision-afflicted knows that things are wrong, but knows not why.

The inheritance of knowledge is danger. Let the timid flee. Even immortals fear what a man can know.

EVERY person alive today exists within a prison realm designed to deceive them that they are free, when they are not. Yes, our world is beautiful. It has to be... there is deceit in the design. We are MORE than we suppose ourselves to be, able to break free of this programming and accomplished incredible things.

I am 44 years old at the time of this writing, having walked through this clever dungeon for the first 40 years of my life, a pawn in another's game. But at 40 years old I emerged with a torch burning sacred fire... a secret. In this book I will lead you through a similar darkness and when we emerge at the end you'll find your own torch lit with a similar flame. Beware, ere I lead you to the light I'll have to drag you through the mire.

Oliver Wendell Holmes said that when the human mind is stretched by a new idea it can never go back to its original dimensions. This is the value of learning, of absorbing new information from diverse sources. Public education saps the initiative, waters down what needs to be highlighted. It levels the plateau of intellectual development, while striving to make equals of everyone... a control mechanism no different than organized religion. Both serve the same purpose.

Our secular selves are taught that all mysteries are solved and that we are in control; our spiritual selves are quarantined with antiquated systems of thought made acceptable because the dictates were the words of a god. Both conceal the truth – we are NOT in control in the collective, and our predicament is not the work of any deity. If the God of Judeo-Christianity truly wrote the Bible and made the world what it is today then any rational individual having reviewed the evidence will rightly determine that God is an enemy of mankind. And this, written by myself, comes from a man who spent the first 40 years of his life as a stringent, washed-in-the-blood southern Baptist. Born again, twice-baptized, I have read the entire Bible through over fifty times in my life and have the notes to prove it.

Learning forces us to undergo an intellectual transformation and this is what makes the student open to all types of knowledge quite dangerous to the Establishment – our thoughts lay the foundations to future conditions. Knowledge acquired changes us in subtle ways. We are told, warned actually, by great mentalists long ago, that a little learning is a dangerous thing. The more I distance myself from the core programming that had ensnared me most of my life, the more I appreciate this statement. Now, with long experimentation, imagination, discovery, and implementation of various systems of thought I can clearly see by virtue of retrospect that all my life I experienced only those major events that I set in motion.

My life has not been measured from destination to destination, by periods of peace or discord, stability or chaos, stagnation or accomplishment. No, these are merely aspects of my space-time passage. My life has been measured by conscious decisions, the milestones of my existence being the exercise of discretion to either believe or disbelieve. Over the years I have maintained meticulous records detailing the events of my life, which enabled me to see a definitive pattern between my attitude and my experiences. It is axiomatic that one's attitude is but a personality's outward manifestation of the condition of the mind. This being so, and demonstrated many times in my life, then I must conclude that I have never suffered anything other than what I expected to endure, my expectations a projection, mentally reflected back to me as circumstances.

The New Thought movement, or Positive Thought movement, based on the law of attraction and theory that a positive mind produces positive experiences, has worked for many individuals. But equally, it has been ineffective for others. There is a reason for this that I will reveal to you, a flaw in the formula that will be rectified herein.

I have never been surprised by anything that I have experienced, be it positive or negative. With the conditions of my life derived from my own psyche, I am left with no one to blame but myself.

As a deist, a student of the Gnosis, I hold that God is a part of our reality. But as an anti-religionist I accept that he is still unknown to us. The creature and Creator are One, and the interface between them is mental. We pray and never receive because the architecture of our 4th-dimensional existence mandates that men do not receive what they want, but what they *are*. Edgar Cayce said that what a man thinks continually, he becomes. A lot about Cayce I dislike, but we agree on that one.

Here are some quotes from men that I have a great affinity toward:

"LET A MAN RADICALLY ALTER
HIS THOUGHTS, AND HE WILL
BE ASTONISHED AT THE RAPID
TRANSFORMATION IT WILL EFFECT IN
THE MATERIAL CONDITIONS OF HIS
LIFE. MEN IMAGINE THAT THOUGHT
CAN BE KEPT SECRET, BUT IT CANNOT;
IT RAPIDLY CRYSTALLIZES INTO
HABIT, AND HABIT SOLIDIFIES INTO
CIRCUMSTANCE." — JAMES ALLEN

"I AM MORE THAN I SUPPOSE MYSELF
TO BE, AND PERHAPS ALL THOSE
PERFECTIONS WHICH I ATTRIBUTE TO
GOD ARE IN SOME WAY POTENTIALLY IN
ME." — RENE DESCARTES

"DO NOT EXPECT GOD TO DO FOR US
WHAT HE CAN ONLY DO THROUGH US."
— THOMAS TROWARD (1909)

"EXPECTATION IS A FORCE, EXPECT
THE BEST TO HAPPEN... ONE WHO
HAS LEARNED TO TRUST WILL NOT
BE SURPRISED EVEN WHEN HE FINDS
THINGS COMING FROM THE MOST
UNEXPECTED SOURCES." — ERNEST
HOLMES (1919)

When one dissolves Christianity of its dressings, this teaching, this ideology of faith, is clearly found... that our physical reality is a mere reflection of inner ideas and convictions. Even Jesus in the Gospel narratives never healed anyone. Heed what Jesus said when others were healed who had come to him –

"ACCORDING TO YOUR FAITH BE IT
UNTO YOU." —Matthew 9:29

"THY FAITH HATH MADE THEE WHOLE."
—Matthew 9:20, 22

"RECEIVE THY SIGHT, THY FAITH HATH
SAVED THEE." —Luke 18:42

"BE NOT AFRAID, ONLY BELIEVE." —Mark
5:36

Chapter Three

DEFINING ONE'S PATH

I know who I am and understand my place as I journey through this little corner of existence. As author of www. archaix.com, it is important that you know I am no "holier-than-thou" type, no pompous moron stuck up with learning. I'm a good ol' boy who just happens to have a strange gift for memorizing things that interest me. At 40 years old I was awakened. With the veil torn away, I was made to see with clarity that everything I had studied for years had a focus, a direction. That the religious programming that had me stuck, over and over again, was a spiritual poison camouflaged as freedom. A programming of absolute genius – to mask a dungeon with illusory trappings, and then blame its inmates for its existence.

I am comfortable with who I am, an admixture of good and evil, a divided soul ever analyzing its other half, suspended between the holy and profane. A moralist, yes, but I still retain a capacity for wickedness (a well-known human trait that I recognize and admit to). One can use it for good. It is this ever-influencing of opposite attractions that builds character, our personas molded by our constant decisions.

If you want to fully understand the nature of reality and how we create circumstances governing our lives, if you want to know the precise mental formula you need in order to change the conditions of your life, then you are no different than I was not long ago. Your search ends here.

Exhaustive research in comparative religions old and new, in occult and magical systems, in philosophical systems oriental and occidental, and in stringent analysis of multidisciplinary scientific experimentation of all things perceivable, has forced upon us the demonstrable fact that reality is not real at all, that the physical is but a figment of the collective imagination, that all things phenomenal are but phantasms of a hive psyche. It has for over a century been known to science that the magnification of any solid material object reveals great distances of nothingness between objects like electrons and nuclei, and that electrons orbit far away from their nucleic host, and can change from wave forms to solid phenomena when observed. A physical object is distinguished from another only by the number of orbiting electrons. These atomic distances microscopically mirror their macroscopic counterparts – Earth as an electron is 93 million miles away from its nucleic Sol, and in the space between is nothing. Our sun is 4.2 light years from the closest stellar system, Alpha Centauri/Proxima. The distances between tiny nuclei are comparable to stars, but when a nucleus is magnified enough we finally reach the foundation of physicality... an oscillating field. Pure energy with no physical property. Inside all material objects is more empty space than solid, and the core solid nuclei are in essence miniscule entanglements of suspended energy. The world of existence is a property of perception. To believe we are physical beings in a material medium is tantamount to describing a breeze passing through fog.

From of old there are whispers. Hidden teachings borne from east to west, a secret ever known to but a few. The world is a complex construct, a prison of physicality designed to confine souls in an aura of sense-perception so perfectly fashioned as to deceive the imprisoned spirit. A dungeon realm of the Demiurge is this holosphere. Immortal beings in quarantine by an enemy in a prison of unknown origin designed to make its captives believe that they are a part of the Creation, when they have actually been cut off. Held in place by a powerful, diabolical mind. Its victims immortal, they cannot be killed. So this Demiurge, the god of this world of sense-perception, a creation of his own design, invented a way to deceive eternal beings into believing they were mortal, that in living they now had to fear death.

This entity is not omnipotent. It is not a creator, but a manipulator. A human soul awakens, perceives the holospheric illusions for what they are, and then creates one's own interference patterns, freed from the confines of ignorance. Thus the man is no longer a marionette. This sinister mind, the enemy, has no more power over the freed individual, who then writes their own destiny. Immersed in this thought medium, the living souls are asleep. But one who awakens knows the holosphere for what it is – a mirror. This spirit projects his will, modifies the medium to conform to his wants, changes reality. He is a creator whom the destroyer no longer deceives.

We think in terms of gender and genera, polarizing everything passing through our sense-range. The acute mind knows that discoveries are not made by seeking similarities. We are prone to draw conclusions from the recognition of correlates. In this way we search the surface of phenomena without seeing its depth. To truly learn about a thing is to identify its distinctions, isolate disparities and see why it is dissimilar. Unfortunately, both methods of analysis merely reinforce the holospheric matrix that deceives us into believing in distinctions between things and concepts that really don't exist.

Anything we accept as true, in essence becomes a trap, a model of confinement. One who looks at the world from inside his model can only interpret data through this sphere of belief-objectivity, which is impossible from within a believed worldview. The observer is trapped in subjective analysis, though he believes he is objective. A man inside a bubble thinks his vision is clear though he must view things through this film, a watery lens that reflects back some light, but distorts reflections due to its spheric curvature.

The man is oblivious of his prison. The outside world only partially influences him because the bubble reflects away data and phenomena he would have ordinarily perceived from a different vantage point.

The reality matrix is sufficiently complex enough to induce us to believe in it. The demon chaser finds demons, the dowser discovers water, the religionist sees reasons everywhere that give proof to his faith, as the witch who knows she miscast her spell then suffers for it. The astronomer ever discovers more distance galaxies to replace prior universal boundaries first known only in theory, and the UFO researcher finds proof of extraterrestrials in testimonies, in video, on film, in ancient art, texts and even in biblical imagery.

Both the heliocentricist and the Flat Earther can separately provide "evidence" that our world is either a globe hurtling through space or a flat plane covered by a dome, neither aware that they are both as equally right as they are wrong. Immersed within this holofield, this deceptive medium continually reflects back as evidence those projections sent into it. Wherever there are people to believe in something, the holosphere will provide evidence of its existence. Seek and ye shall find is a trap. Philosophies, faiths, and conclusions of science are all supported by evidence, proofs and convictions, but all are in opposition to one another. Reality is then a misnomer, disguised as duality. Existence is a confluence of realities in myriads of superimposed minds – a multiplicity of surveyors observing architecture of their own collective construction. Only in a hologram can contrary realities coexist without contact.

Remember this fact. The architecture of our reality frames meaning to fictions just as much as facts.

We are more than we suppose ourselves to be, gods and goddesses in the making, oppressed in a world we live within, but it is not our true home. The power to CHANGE reality, to CREATE new circumstances in our lives, is the greatest secret this prison realm seeks to obscure. We have the power to draw from ourselves MORE than we contain... do you know how?

We are a species in love with our illusions, deigning to admit realities that only exist within ourselves.

Physics calculations have long shown us the mathematical echoes of a higher dimension (beyond our holosphere) but these same models blind us to the holospheric nature of reality. As intellectual subroutines embedded into a complex interactive program, a data cloud, we humans do not have the sensorial apparatus necessary to perceive the actual unreality of our existence. It is with great difficulty for subjective sentience to objectively analyze an environment that it is suspended within. We are malleable software immersed in to a vastly more intricate programmed illusion. Unable to distinguish the real from the imagined, the imaginary becomes real to us. What we accept as true becomes one with our programming and all "facts" and phenomena experienced afterwards tends to reinforce what we have accepted as true. It is with the greatest difficulty for us to break away, to question or disbelieve something that we formerly held as true. With religion it is devastating. Belief in any religion reinforces the hold of the prison matrix.

We are also trapped by faith in any science or discovery as absolutes, trust in human institutions, or the thought of racial disparities or national differences. They all serve to strengthen the believability of the holospheric programs modified anciently by a wicked mind, but now reinforced moment-by-moment by the billions of people trapped in this persuasive reality matrix. Once we are programmed to believe in any faith, especially a religious one, all information received through sense-perception is filtered through a worldview that supports the religious model. A disturbing fact of the religionist mindset tends to regard persons of variant belief systems to be no longer viewed as individuals – but rather as lesser parts of their environment, less real, heathens, or simply inhuman. All too often, peaceful religionists-turned-homicidal fanatics have justified murder as a holy right.

The stunning achievement of one who recognizes his own programming flaws finds that in disbelieving what he formerly held as true now affects many other areas of his worldview. Absolutes now blur into uncertainties. His belief had fundamentally altered the way he processed information and the holosphere modified what it brought in contact with him because it only reflects what is projected into it.

Reality reinforces belief no matter if the programming is right or wrong. This is why so few who are devout religionists have ever broken free of their thought-model. To the faithful, to doubt is to backslide. Their belief is a moral issue with walls built around change or the idea of change. The fears of apostasy, heresy, and independent thought of any kind looms over them, silently menacing their inner lives, whether they are conscious of it or not. Their program has become a trap, but to resist it is to threaten their very afterlife – to disbelieve formerly accepted religious programming is to shake the very foundations of a person's psyche.

Chapter Four

SECRETS TO GUARD AND EMPLOY

Herein lies a profound secret, a truth largely unknown and ignored. A property of reality that can be exploited to our benefit. In nature, that which harms can also heal. Religionist projections induce reality to reflect back expected conditions. The holosphere responds to beliefs projected upon it. Not mere thoughts, which are fleeting, but convictions. Convictions affect behavior, habits, conduct and speech, which form probability molds that echo through space-time to reflect back as circumstances. Thoughts of themselves are insufficient – changing what is to what one wants to be requires belief. It has been said that a belief is not merely as idea the mind possesses, but an idea that possesses the mind. We always think; we are mental creatures. This common denominator is what unifies the religionist to the magi. Both have their unique beliefs and both see the results of their faith operative in reality.

The same confinement programming used to direct and control our trajectory through the holosphere can be employed to our advantage – and with astonishing results. Acceptance of a belief system by an individual frames the holosphere into circumstances conforming to expected norms. But for every new thing learned, the acceptance of a new vantage point, all previously known frames of reference shift to align with the new data. Not only does the acceptance of something alter one's reality, but the changing also affects the individual. There is an interface between perceiver and perceived. An exchange of information. An element of sentience pervades reality; we exist as both pawn and player.

The bonds that deceive us are our bounty as well. In a world full of victims the victor is rare. Most people live their lives in a reactive mindset, recognizing conditions, conforming to obvious probabilities and totally experiencing an existence of effects all stimulated by external causes. In the holospheric probability cloud we are ghosts immersed in a fog, the substance of possibilities just as real as the cloud that contains us. Flowing with a current, the fish suddenly turns out of the stream, changes direction, and water (the world of the fish) is moved. But people are conditioned to follow, to obey programming dictates, to conform. Few come to the awareness of the power of human actions to create conditions because of the holosphere's perpetuity programming.

Our everyday, mundane reality has a way of perpetuating its routine continuity. When the abnormal is not expected the normal continues. The cycle is powerful because the victim-perceiver of the world observes no change in present circumstances, so accepts reality as it is, and thus continues it. By accepting present conditions as they are, one receives these same present conditions in the future. This is bondage. Existing is not the same as living. To be free of undesirable circumstances one must imagine life without them. To have wealth, one must envision enjoying activities that require it. To have discretion, one must imagine exercising it. Fortune favors the bold because to be bold is to know one possesses strength for what is necessary. The bold change their environment because they are NOT bound by circumstance. To be bold one must have vision and this inner mental picture is then projected onto the screen of the holosphere to become reality reflected back as the conditions and circumstances of one's life. Though the meek may inherit the earth, it is always the bold who rule it.

Accept this singular tenet and your world will change. You will become a concentration of vast creative potential, an auric field saturated with all of the knowledge and power acquired in life, ready to be drawn upon at will – a vortex that pulls people and favored circumstances to you through the illusionary barriers of time-space. Nothing can be beyond the reach of your will. No boundaries exist because all is connected. Your power will be magnified in patience and trust, knowing that events, circumstances and things are instantly moved by your thoughts, aligning toward you by repetitive thinking in the positive... drawn more and more into your life through daily streams of thought and expectation. As your daily behavior reflects these thoughts, what you want begins manifesting in your life. The holospheric Oversoul will both obey the master or afflict the slave; the master has all he wants and builds his own life, the slave remains adrift in a chaotic sea of thought-constructs belonging to others.

By observation and sense-perception we interact with the holospheric environment and it is strengthened around us by our awareness. Indeed, our own biology is a part of the bonds that confine us. As a mental construct, the holosphere is influenced mentally by the individuals within it. We write our own code, all too often prejudiced by circumstance. But in living out our own program, authors of our own fate, none can blame God. The problem we must address is our own reaction to external stimuli, a surrounding world saturated with negativity.

We rage, bitter and resentful, observing our environs and recognizing that things are out of order, that the undeserving are promoted, the worthy unrewarded, innocents are condemned, and the mighty are subdued. Those with acuity are cursed, while halfwits are happiest. In constant contact with reality's inequities, a conditioning molds us into accepting the world as an environment where this is the norm, the expected. This is the greatest aspect of the holospheric Law of Attraction operable in our every day lives, the Law of Reflection in its most potent form. Recognition of its operation will be necessary to the complete reversal of the negative circumstances of one's life. Every time we are angry, sad, unhappy, discontent, impatient or destitute over a condition in our life we are reinforcing its continuance... the PRESENT mental output molds present conditions onto the architecture of the future. We are SO POWERFUL and too blind to see that we walk roads of our own construction.

Remember always – we receive not what we want but what we are, a truth misunderstood by the religionists who break themselves on the rack of prayer. By being patient, content, hopeful, aware that our wants are possible, we strongly attract those conditions. By keeping a firm mental picture of what you want to experience, your positive attitude will begin altering the circumstances of your life, the holosphere shifting reality to align with your thought and emotions. Negative expectations produce negative results. This phenomenon is observed all the time. Such a law must have its counterpart – positive expectations produce positive results.

The notion that our fears are reflected back upon us is merely an example of the Law of Reality at work, not a law in and of itself. Fears weigh heavily on the mind penetrating the very fabric of our personality. Fears occupy our mental life with a steady stream of thought, amplified by biological reactions of anxiety.

The reality matrix we are immersed in is not our enemy, it is our own programming. We are conditioned to doubt, fear, disbelieve and 99% of humanity are enslaved in an intricate sphere of overlapping reflections that harmonize to reinforce what is doubted, feared or believed. What is true of fear and anxiety is equally true of a positive mind – a calm, excited expectation draws mental desires into physical experience, just as terrible things are attracted to the one who fears them. We are the Law, an insignificant piece of vast potential, a creative spark able to illuminate its own path. Where there exists even a tiny amount of creative force, we can always be assured that we are immersed in an infinite medium of transformative power so malleable that it is mentally moved.

So in changing your attitude you change your world. You will know when your frequency has changed. After a spell of suppressing negativity in your thinking, things will occur that *should* upset you, but do not. You are no longer in resonance with the negative and VERY QUICKLY your positive attitude then causes positive things to manifest out of negative situations.

The power of the mind to manipulate reality, to induce change, has been noted in various ways by many famous and lesser-known people. It is important to know what others have said on this topic.

Emotion unveils in the soul of man the development of powers so deeply hidden that by the majority of men their very existence is denied. —P.D. Ouspensky

The man who can sincerely thank God for the things which as yet he owns only in imagination, has the real faith. —Wallace D. Wattles, 1910

Expect the best to happen... one who has learned to trust will not be surprised even when he finds things coming from the most unexpected sources. —Ernest Holmes, 1919

Dream lofty dreams, and as you dream, so shall you become. Your vision is the promise of what you shall one day be. —Baltasar Gracian

This is our divine birthright – nothing hinders but ourselves. —Ernest Holmes, 1919

Man himself in part creates the conditions under which he lives, and is not merely the impotent prisoner of circumstance. —Lewis Mumford

The world is as we imagine it. The world is as we perceive it because we have been created by the world for the purpose of observing and understanding it. —Gerhard Staguhn

What one thinks continually, he becomes. —Edgar Cayce

Whether you think you can or think you can't, either way you're right. —Henry Ford

A person who sees what he wants to see, regardless of what appears, will some day experience in the outer what he so faithfully sees within. —Ernest Holmes, 1919

We receive not what we want but what we are. —James Allen

When you look at your current state of affairs and define yourself by that, then you doom yourself to have nothing more than the same in the future. —James Ray

The divine man knows that faith itself is not conceived and known, but lived and enacted. —Anonymous

Because we are what we are, we may become what we will. —James Allen

Fate is in our hands... the whole trouble has been that we reason as men and not as gods. —Ernest Holmes, 1919

A change of world view can change the world viewed. —Joseph Chilton Pierce

The man who does not believe in miracles makes it certain that he will never partake in one. —William Blake

Men are anxious to improve their circumstances, but are unwilling to improve themselves; they therefore remain bound. —James Allen

One cannot solve a problem with the same kind of thinking that gave rise to the problem. —Albert Einstein (quoted from Ervin Laszlo blog)

The answer to prayer is not according to your faith while you are talking, but according to your faith while you are working. —Wallace D. Wattles, 1910

If the end is already secured, then it follows that all the steps leading to it are secured also. —Thomas Troward

No one is powerless, ordinary or insignificant. To claim so is to claim that divine infinity is all of those things. If we change our imagination of ourselves we can live as the incarnate ocean and not as the disconnected droplet; as infinity and not only as far as the eyes can see. —David Icke

It is shameful to be alive and not live. —Victor Hugo

People don't see the world as it really is, even if they had the intelligence, they don't have the desire. —C.W. Dalton

Most men occasionally stumble over the truth, but they pick themselves back up and continue on as if nothing happened. —Winston Churchill

The search for reality is the most dangerous of all undertakings for it destroys the world in which you live. —Nisargadatta Maharaj

Look at your world and your life and you are looking at what you think of yourself at the very core of your being... the subconscious creates a physical replica of itself before our eyes, in people, places and experiences which reflect its sense of self. At any moment in any day, we are casting around us a magnetic image of what we think of ourselves. It is this which creates our reality by magnetically attracting to us experiences which correspond with that pattern. —David Icke

Reality is veiled... we are prisoners of an inner world, of a machine that produces a virtual reality. So it ends that the senses – our only means of contact with the external world, keep us separated from it through representations that are not real. —Massimo Citro

All the major thinkers have rightly perceived that bodies are illusions, representations of something else and what

we call existence is rather like a dream. But this secret has been hidden, transmitted only to those able to accept the terrible truth that we live in a fiction. —Massimo Citro

Reality remains unknowable to us while we cling to our illusions. —Helen D. Vandeman, *Reality Is But a Dream*

If anybody's a wizard, everybody is, to some degree, a wizard. —Charles Fort, 1932

What the mind has created only the mind can undo. —Buddha

The truth is to know that everything is an illusion. —Professor John Wu

Where the cause is, there is the remedy. —James Allen

People who live in fear of disease are the people who get it. —James Allen

Thoughts are things... and each thing creates its kind. —Ella Wheeler Wilcox

Faith or fear... where one is found, the other cannot exist. —Napolean Hill

The victim mentality creates the victim reality. —David Icke

I receive that God and I are one... I am then an immovable cause that moves all things. —Meister Ekhart, 13th cent. Dominican

If you think there is opposition, then opposition will appear. —Anonymous

An above listed quote of the erudite Charles Fort on wizards provides us a totally unique vantage point by which to reanalyze this data. The believer in a faith attributes the answering of prayer to their deity, or, as I presume, the Infinite Oversoul merely reflects back in the physical what we project mentally. That material reality is actually an illusion of physicality I term the holosphere. This also seems to be the idea behind ancient and more contemporary magical systems.

Chapter Five

THE MAGIC OF THE MIND

What separates the magus from the breadth of humanity is the knowledge of a single secret... awareness of the existence of the ether, an invisible essence permeating all things in space and time. Even spanning beyond the past and after the future.

As the Absolute, the ether is an infinitely impressionable medium, a mirror reflecting what is known and believed, a purely impersonal force amenable to suggestion that instantly begins modifying reality to conform to expectations projected in to it.

The magus knows that the Absolute is the source of all we want, therefore, in knowing this, the Absolute becomes the source of all we want because this etheric reality is actually a magical construction so baffling to scientists they mask it under the descriptions of quantum camouflage.

There have always been magi, seers and oracles of old, prophets and sages separated from the sea of humanity by their acute intuition, knowing that the unseen is clearly evident in those things we can see.

The learned magus knows that –

> present reality does not actually exist – it is a shadow of something else that is real.

> nothing is absolutely true and everything is permitted.

> good and evil are irrelevant, neither can be an absolute.

> LIVING is the purpose of life.

> belief is a tool for achieving effects.

> we are the Law and life's conditions are effects.

> in the ether there is no distance between we and what we desire.

> reality reflects the personality impressed upon it – if this personality is a wizard then wizardry will result.

> we are more than we suppose ourselves to be.

> we are more than anything that can happen to us.

> in creating new conditions the magus is in no way limited by precedent.

> the positive mind produces power just as the negative one negates it.

> all potential lies in our insignificance.

> the best way to predict the future is to invent it (Alan Kay).

The magi knows what the religionist does not, that *awareness* of power *creates* power. Also –

> to be free of unwanted circumstances, one must imagine life without them.

> reality reflects what we are, not what we deceive ourselves to be.

> life is an echo... what is sent out comes back as a copy of what was sent out.

The religionist prays to God and then claims it is "God's will" when prayers go unanswered, despite it being biblically written – "Ask and ye shall receive."

This is not the way of the magus. The magus lives out his desires by expecting his word fulfilled, and he acts accordingly. His maxims:

> act as though you are, and you will be.

> you are what you repeatedly do.

Chapter Six

DODGING DEAD-ENDS

The religionist is imbued with slave programming, in submitting to deity he denies his own divinity. The religionist is ensnared, not realizing that –

> thinking with restrictions, restricts us.

> thinking there are limitations, limits us.

> negative thinking reinforces negative conditions.

> to think of opposition causes opposition to manifest.

> our fears tend to follow us.

> waiting is anxiety, which serves to push away the very thing waited for.

> active pursuit causes active flight; waiting causes avoidance; only when we halt these actions do we attract things to us.

> the prayer of desperation admits a situation for what it is, and thus *continues it.*

This is the singular greatest tragedy of the human condition. For thousands of years the religious paradigms have trained generation after generation of the faithful to take their burdens to God in fervent prayer, an old scheme designed to harm humanity. These billions of people have inadvertently strengthened the negative influences by admitting these influences existed and that they had no power to alter them. The delusional religionists are trapped in a perpetual cycle of self-destruction. If prayers admitting one's powerlessness truly worked, then the world would be a very different place than it is today. Cancer, crime, hunger, natural disasters, disease, poverty – these continue unabated into the twenty-first century because the many, through their belief, continue this negative empowerment.

But this was not written for them. This was written for those who dare to choose their own reality tunnel, to forge their own path through holospheric reality. You DO NOT HAVE TO CONFORM. This is not a world of absolutes. You are not a wolf just because you refuse to be a sheep. Let the lemmings run while you stop to get your bearings.

Let them fill the sea while you stand on firm ground, observing your terrain more clearly.

Prayer is the method of the religionist. The condition of our present world *proves* that the religionist version of prayer does *not* work.

The knower of the TRUTH wastes no time pondering over outcomes, knowing that by seeking to do more is an admission that one has not done enough. He understands clearly that –

> to seek more learning can be an impediment to *knowing.*

> one who knows the truth *seeks no more.*

> a matter that becomes clear, ceases to concern us. (Frederick Nietzsche)

> the knower is united with the *known.*

> letting go of what we want is the only way to get it.

> where the Oversoul guides, *it provides.*

> we are entitled in life to whatever we have the audacity to claim.

The shamanism of the simple culture is little different than the faith of the believer and the sorceries of the magi. The pompous scientist regards these other forms of reality arrogantly, as being beneath his intellectual dignity. But are they? An Oversoul, Gaia, Maya, the Absolute, the ether, the All Father, Cosmic Consciousness... and then we have the holosphere. So many nicely packaged theories, misnomers, we fail to truly see things objectively, within the big picture of the holosphere, so we invent an explanation. Aside from the holosphere, all are wrong in explaining the collective as a whole, but are absolutely correct in the particular – because they reflect the holosphere when viewed correctly. Interesting how holograms work – that a slight adjustment of one's vantage point suddenly unveils realms of other actualities.

Chapter Seven

GENERATING EVENTS

Whether men know it or not, their *actions*, reinforced by thought, cast waveforms of *information* on trajectories into the future. Every day men are immersed in a deceitful medium bent on forging *fantasy into reality.* The blind live subjectively under the conditions caused by *others;* the knowing observer BUILDS the world through want and *imagination,* for the holosphere best propagates *truths through lies,* absorbing *fictions* to reflect them into physical reality as *facts.*

The majority spend their lives inside the mirrored maze; the few move *beyond its confines* through different corridors. A knowledge of these unseen paths affords one the ability to not only predict an outcome, but also *cause* a future event.

The future on a *personal* level is not fixed, however, quantum pathways of information *relative* to past events

ARE FIXED. These are *potentia*, the possible paths your life can take. There are multiple electron streams in a storm, but at a single instance of time lightning manifests through only one or two of these paths. All potentia existed for many directions but vanished once lightning (nature) chose a conduit that bridged the *nonexistent* (fiction) to existence (fact).

The principle message of quantum mechanics, according to physicist Henry Stapp, is that the world is *not* determined by initial conditions, once and for all; every event of measurement is potentially *creative* and may open new possibilities. Quantum nonlocality, the existence of a thing suspended *outside* of time-space, reveals that the fundamental process of nature lies outside space-time but *generates events* than can be *located in space-time.*

The quantum nature of brainwave activity and our cerebral interfacing with the *not-real-becoming-real-reality* is the reason events are generated along pathways that only *appear* random to those who are unaware of the space-time mathematics of potentia. The problem for scientists is that they are observing and trying to describe effects due to something which they refuse to believe can exist (magical structure of reality). The problem for magicians is that they refuse to believe that the *effects they create* or observe are due to something for which *equations could be written.* For this wisdom we owe *Liber Kaos* (page 40).

Every scientific explanation of reality is at its core a *belief,* an intellectual theology. Just as there are multitudes of variant and some opposing denominations of Christianity, so too are there violently-in-opposition schools of scientific thought. Scientists in opposing disciplines all consider themselves scientists who believe they know the truth in their respective fields. However, the "truths" of opposing fields remain true to each of those scientists who have observed, studied, discovered and documented them, despite the fact that these "truths" don't often match between disciplines. We live in an infinite medium that generates "proofs" for ANYTHING HELD TO BE TRUE.

The etheric medium encourages events similar in nature to follow certain paths (potentia). By *intent* and *desire*, with an AWARENESS of what we are doing, we can easily influence events BEFORE nature has made up her mind. Paths of potentia are time-space GATES, influenced by the mental to the material. KNOWING this operation affords one great power in *selecting* the most favored timing or outcome. One person making up their minds can do it. Two or more people acting in concert can achieve astonishing results. We as *thinking*, emotional beings exercising *intent* with expectation can –

1. modify/alter future activity of systems/individuals.

2. create new circumstances/conditions *where none existed before.*

Casting thought projections well in advance allows a greater chance of influencing favored potentia. Further, *creativity* and *imagination* possess powers of their own. Creativity builds reality, while acceptance merely continues it. Universal holospheric reflection is shown in that –

> our existence maintains the magical property of *confirming* most of the interpretations placed upon it. (*Liber Kaos*, page 191)

> it has an obliging nature, reflexive, providing proof for any cosmological scheme, scientific or mystical, foisted upon it. (*Giants of Gaia,* Mann & Sutton)

> theories tend to attract their own proof. (*The Secrets of the Stones*, page 18)

> it has the property of tending to provide evidence for, and confirmation of, whatever paradigm one chooses to believe in. (*Liber Kaos*, page 56)

Our holospheric medium is stimulated into activity by the *beliefs* of those confined within it, a morphic field that continually generates the real out of the imagined. The architecture of reality is so plastic in receptivity that it will always produce effects in proportion to the waveforms of our cerebral transmitters. The secret is so simple: *act* as if you *are,* and you *will be.*

Chapter Eight

AFFIRMATIONS

I have made a long study of the events of my life and the world around me, allowing me to make these inescapable conclusions –

MY EXPERIENCES CONFORM TO *MY* PICTURE OF REALITY, MY BELIEFS. THE OUTCOME OF MY ENDEAVORS CORRELATE WITH MY *EXPECTATION*. THEREFORE –

> my assumptions of truth, *become* the truth.

> manifesting what I believe is the *function* of the Universe.

> the world has no power over me – it merely reflects what I choose to see, confirming my beliefs about myself, which obey no laws, nor are they confined by them.

> at all times I am casting out a magnetic image of what I think of myself, attracting to me experiences that correspond with that image; my *self-perception* creates circumstances that *confirm* my image of myself; the world responds to me in the *precise proportion* of how I perceive myself.

BECAUSE WE LIVE IN A FICTION, WHICH IS A PRODUCT OF THE *IMAGINATION*, I CREATE MY OWN REALITY. MY PERCEPTIONS OF NATURAL PHENOMENA AND LAWS OF PHYSICS ARE CREATIONS OF OUR COLLECTIVE MINDS THAT I HAVE ACCEPTED – BUT AM NOT BOUND BY THEM, FOR I EXIST MENTALLY IN A DIMENSION *BEYOND* THE MATERIAL. THEREFORE –

> I conjure events into existence by my desire to experience them.

> I encourage events to move in a certain direction.

> I alter one reality to create another in order to make things happen that would not ordinarily occur.

> I draw people, events and conditions from unexpected sources.

> I originate new conditions *out of nothing.*

> I set things in motion that do not diminish over time.

> I live out the fiction to create the fact.

> I change the physical world through practiced *intention.*

BECAUSE 100% OF THE FUTURE IS CONSTRUCTED OF A UNION OF THE *REAL* AND THE *IMAGINED*, I DREAM MY LIFE INTO EXISTENCE, FREE TO CREATE ANY REALITY I PREFER. THEREFORE, –

> my creativity possesses powers of its own.

> my thoughts collapse possibilities into realities.

> morphing from one self to another, switching reality tunnels, I instantly induce reality to change – with each self I assume, I bring about an *alternate universe.*

> existing in a state of nonunion, I exercise power over my environment.

> *independent* of existence, I am able to employ any magical technology I will, from my own entirely subjective, complete and closed system.

> my own self-created subjective reality is a by-product of my *imagination*, both entertaining and profiting me.

> I deliberately act *beforehand* to create virtual influences, imaginings that then *modify reality.*

EVERYTHING TO ME IS POSSIBLE AND REAL BECAUSE IT IS ALL MOORED TO AN ILLUSION –THE HOLOSPHERE.   I AM MOORED TO A LIVING, ETHERIC FIELD, *NOT* THE PERCEIVED REALITY TUNNELS.   BECAUSE I AM A SPARK AMIDST AN INFINITE SEA OF POSSIBILITY –

> my experiences are due to the reality tunnels I choose to view the world through.

> I create experiences by inventing new reality tunnels.

> I *imagine* the things I desire in order to build *informed fields* that imprint the ether, drawing them into my physical existence.

DUE TO THESE REALIZATIONS I CONCLUDE WITH THIS SUMMARY THAT –

> products of my imagination are not limited by precedent.

> in the ether, everything I want *already exists.*

> *knowing* there is no opposition, opposition can *not appear.*

> *nothing* hinders but myself.

> my thoughts of power *produce* power.

> by acts of imagination I draw from my self *more than I contain.*

> my faith is not conceived and known, but *lived* and *enacted.*

> by acting as though I am, *I become.*

> by my attitude I influence all outcomes.

> when I change my attitude I change my world.

> what my mind most contemplates, that I become.

> I receive not what I want, but what *I am.*

> because I am what I am, I become what *I will.*

Chapter Nine

GENERAL GUIDELINES

Sad, this preconditioned, programmed mindset we humans suffer – that we require formulas and step-by-step procedures to achieve results. As one who walked in your shoes I understand your need and will give you such an itinerary.

Because thoughts are *things*, they are the builders of our future existence. All of the thoughts of collective humanity in the past have constructed our present. But our present existence can be altered by thinking about what we want and *acting* as if things had *already* changed. Here is your formula:

IMAGINE what you want, understanding that the past means *nothing*. Imagining requires the intent that there will be a fulfillment. Fantasizing does NOT manifest reality, a million daydreams still lack the impulse of belief. Do not imagine *how* things are to come to pass, that is the domain of the Universe/ Ether/ Spirit/ Holosphere/ Oversoul.

SPEAK and WILL your wants into existence by affirming that *I am* this or that, and be aware that the creative power works *through* you even after you've ceased dwelling on your desire. Awareness of power *creates* power.

KNOW THAT IT IS DONE by realizing that what is wanted EXISTS NOW. When we accept something as real it becomes real to us. The Universe is a mirror of space and time, creating every day what is *known...* reflecting back into the present world what was *projected into it.*

BE GRATEFUL, thank your God, feel gratitude for having already received what is wanted. When you can genuinely be thankful for things you have yet to possess, you demonstrate pure FAITH, and will receive whatever it is you want.

LET GO OF YOUR DESIRE by calmly trusting that it will come to pass. When we desire something it *avoids* us in both space and time because longing and desire always contains an element of doubt, strengthening those conditions that brought on longing and desire. Lingering doubt blocks out the possibility of success, so letting go of the desire and waiting for success is the highest trust one can have toward your God.

ACT as though YOU ARE, and you WILL BE. Your daily life, your *actions,* must supplement belief. Work to realize your wants and let God do the rest.

NEVER concentrate on what you do NOT WANT TO HAPPEN because fear is emotionally charged and what is feared will always be reflected back as *conditions.* When we think with restrictions, we are *restricted.* When we project limitations, we are *limited.* Remember, the prayer of desperation admits a situation for what IT IS, and thus *continues it.*

You can become an unstoppable engine of productivity by simply *doing.* The very act of being productive is a *projection* of activity imprinted on the holosphere that echoes back to the present, giving you things to do to maintain *productivity.* A woman staring at a blank screen is doing nothing; she is not in resonance with what she wants to do. By changing directions and *doing* something else for a while, her mind will later be deluged with ideas for her to begin typing onto that screen. The best way to handle writer's block is to do something else. LET GO. Stasis only produces stasis.

Chapter Ten

THE GREAT MAXIM:
KNOW THYSELF

The only qualifications I needed to write this material was the pattern of my life. The greatest leaps are made by those who strip away the gloss to see themselves as they really are. Only one who truly knows who they are can know others better than they know themselves. I know me, and have little difficulty describing me to you.

> I am knowledgeable; and yet, I cannot fathom how little I know.

> I am evil; and yet, being evil I am compassionate, with morals.

> I am good; and yet, being good I enjoy also my wickedness.

> I am devilish and divine; and yet, I have favor with God.

> I am powerful; and yet, my strength is not my own.

> I am irreligious; and yet, my spirituality is secure.

> I am creative; and yet, with words I destroy.

> I am destructive; and yet, my words do bring healing.

> I am a man; and yet, I am as immortal as God.

We humans were given power, authority and dominion over an existence that responds to our every thought. When man *thinks*, the Universe pays attention. When man *speaks*, the echo of his *intent* reverberates throughout the whole Creation. When man *acts*, the Universe changes. We are immersed within this creative medium that knows nothing of good and evil, morals, ethics – the ideals of men. It is impersonal and totally amenable to suggestion and absolutely free from precedent. By knowing who I am, the Universe *knows* me, responding by reflecting the reality I project.

What I bind or free, heal or destroy, *becomes* bound or free, healed or destroyed. Our power over men and conditions is due to *awareness* of this liberty. The immediate responsiveness of material reality to our thoughts, words and actions is why those who *know* this are masters amidst this sea of slaves who know not who they are.

By *expecting* my word fulfilled, I *act* accordingly, and it *becomes* fulfilled. By thinking what we want and *acting* as though things had already changed, we transform the mental to the material because we are co-creators with God.

In knowing ourselves it is equally important to recognize fully just what we believe to be true. The very fabric of a person's psyche is totally wrapped around his belief system, his *reality tunnels.* What we truly *believe* does govern our thought processes, our conclusions. We edit away unfavorable, disturbing data all the time because it does not fit into the structure of our paradigm. The choices we make on a daily basis are *not* evidence of free will, but when properly analyzed into their right perspectives, demonstrate that we make choices that comport with our belief systems. This is why it is so important for you to quietly sit down and write out the things you hold to be true. This simple exercise will *awaken you.*

I will not present these ideas in hypocrisy. What I suggest you do, as the reader, is something that I have done for myself. You may not agree with my conclusions, but then again, your reality tunnels are NOT the same as mine. We are each forms of complex "biogramming," suspended within an infinite matrix of *times* and *places* so all-pervasive that your reality tunnels and mine may intersect from time to time, may be totally antithetical to one another, and *never* coalesce. Such is the holographic nature of the Simulacrum.

Chapter Eleven

WHAT I HOLD TO BE TRUE

> Men are not equal. Nature demonstrates that members of the same species are not equals in their social structures.

> Humanity in the collective traverses a FIXED timeline, easily discernable in the occurrences of major events throughout history that transpired according to a fixed geometry of Golden Proportion dimensions (Fibonacci Series) against a passive background of prime numbers; pi, phi, curvature, isometric projections, earth's orbital duration of 365.25 days, axial rotation, obliquity of 23.5 degrees – these are effects of holospheric engineering, the mechanics of a *fixed* system having a terminus.

> Humans as *individuals* are confined within this collective geometry but have the ability to FORGE THEIR OWN FATES, to determine their own *location*

and *circumstances* within this fixed geometrical matrix, a space-time structure that allows movement without itself changing its own dimensions; the swimming of the fish does not change the water.

> We are a solidified reflection of the sum total of our thought activity – as the mind moves, the body follows.

> Through its treacherous topography, geologic instabilities, unpredictable tornadoes, typhoons, tsunamis, windstorms and hurricanes, floods, volcanic eruptions, animal predators, blights, plague, toxic plants and venoms, torrential rain, poisons and even accidents – nature aids in killing men just as it provides him sustenance.

> As a student of the Gnosis, my God is so vast that ten thousand different opinions about Him can all be right.

> My God is so incomprehensible that all the religions of the world cannot describe Him.

> My God is so compassionate that He requires *no one* to fear Him.

> My God is so loving that His touch will end a lifetime of hate.

> My God is unknown, requiring invisible things to perceive Him.

> Christianity promulgates the highest ethical system ever implemented by mankind, however, the Old and New Testament books are proven forgeries, most of the events they depict *never* happened. When eliminating all the fictive historical dressing, these writings are but a collection of the greatest spiritual axioms, quotes, teachings and parables taken from many different cultures and time periods.

> The purpose of life is not the acquisition of knowledge. The more knowledge we acquire, the more we realize we know nothing at all. The purpose of life involves a higher experience totally unconnected with learning mundane material.

> The Universe is saturated with THOUGHT. Many of the thoughts passing through my mind *all the time* are not my own; they are invasive, distracting. Thoughts exist independent of the mind and they *move* through space, or... the thought-field remains *fixed* and it is WE who are moving. I can yield to invasive thoughts and sometimes information saturates me, or I ignore them. They don't go away, but instead change to other thoughts.

> As with the geometrical, palindromic nature of the time-space continuum, *human* nature, its behavior, also remains *fixed*. Though human civilization has advanced to become technologically sophisticated, and has come to recognize the highest ideals and notions in our philosophies, arts and spirituality, we are, at our core, still merely maintaining a civilized veneer covering uncivilized conduct, savagery and willful ignorance. Because human nature is fixed, human actions are predictable.

> Humankind, very long ago, was imbued with slave-programming; we are a *genetic modification* of something else, a sentient life form similar to an older version that was once more powerful. Much of the human genome has been "switched off." These latent genes, so mysterious to the geneticist, hold the key to our destiny, our escape from this holospheric prison. As the containment field we are immersed in weakens, counting down to a definitive terminus, the suppressive force that has kept these myriads of unique genes inactive will collapse and we will BECOME WHO WE REALLY ARE.

> There are academic, scientific, theological and governmental knowledge-filters set in place today to maintain the various status-quos, the current paradigms foisted upon the populace. A tremendous amount of energy and finances have gone into this concerted effort to maintain the popular illusions we cling to, yet many discoveries are made every month that go contrary to what is taught to us, and are *silenced.*

> The news is seldom reported... it is manufactured. News agencies and networks, if truly reporting events, would be in commercial competition with one another to provide innovative, different, compelling news stories to the people instead of reporting all of the same *manufactured* stories on every single broadcast. Creative, meaningful news would induce us to watch their own news shows as opposed to another. But this is not what is occurring. News stations today report the SAME EVENTS, reading from the SAME SCRIPTS while quoting the SAME SOURCES, who all pass around to the people the SAME OPINIONS totally contradicting the idea of objectivity. Even on the local city level the stories are ALL THE SAME from station to station. Example: in the city of Houston there is so

much going on daily that different local stations should NEVER be reporting the same events except for major newsworthy happenings. Our existence is scripted, but YOU do not have to walk this stage. Go by unexpected ways... walk unfrequented paths.

> After over a decade and a half of intense scrutiny into the literature and texts of the ancient world, up to more contemporary times, the following is an *absolute truth* of the human condition. Every race and culture on this planet going back 4000 years to the advent of writing fits within three distinct categories: culture creators, culture bearers and culture destroyers. Every civilization, past and present, can be measured by this standard.

Culture Creators design magnificent judiciary systems and develop highly in the arts and sciences, adding to knowledge and the human experience. They are benefactors to all mankind with a passion for sharing their discoveries around the world. Having many innovative skills, they are mariners, tradesman and builders – people expert at the laying down of infrastructures.

Culture Bearers are those peoples, past and present, who have preserved their way of life over the millennia as a cultural status quo. Rarely are any changes made in technology unless *introduced.* The occasional maverick genius becomes a hero, but the populace does not carry on his vision and his works are often lost. TRADITION and FIXED CULTURE keep these people from any advancement on their own. When in contact with Culture Creators they *thrive,* but revert back to their own culture as soon as the infrastructure collapses from loss of contact.

Culture Destroyers are those who do not belong among the civilization they are found within. Some examples would be marauding Huns or Viking invasions. More subtle forms of them exist today. The Destroyers *change* and *diminish* most everything they come in contact with, having no appreciation, nor understanding, of the brilliance of the institutions they corrupt. Included in all things, they still regard themselves as outsiders. They alter language and the arts, and thrive on the allowances accorded them by their host civilizations – efforts to absorb or peaceably coexist that *never* occur. Culture Destroyers infect a civilization, almost never creating anything of value. By their corruption of the host civilization's values, they eventually turn that civilization into something else.

Every race and culture has participated in being creators, bearers, and destroyers in some capacity. Who plays what roles today is very evident by anyone walking from the sophisticated downtown corporate section, to the inner city neighborhoods, on outward into the affluent suburbs.

And every living soul today has been a participant in these categories through the multitudes of life-simulations they have experienced in their journey to mold their immortal personality.

The beauty of our existence is that no matter *who* we are or *where* we come from, WE DO NOT HAVE TO CONFORM to any of this. You change your frequency, you change your world. Simple as that. The ego, the belief that we are more important than someone else; that we are special while others are not, is a hindrance. Reality reflects what we *are*, not what we deceive ourselves to be. We influence the holosphere to move events in a desired direction until our want is fulfilled. Whether we are seven billion souls living on the thin skin of a planetary sphere, or trapped beneath an illusory heaven on a flat earth, we are afforded great mobility, but not by any singular importance. All potential lies in our *insignificance.*

The average person lives the life that their environment dictates, but the Immortal dictates their life and the *environment obeys...*

I hope you enjoyed this book. I further selfishly hope you tell others, that you write a favorable review, that you *become who you potentially are.* A small book, so I apologize – but it breathes the essence of my soul laid bare. Many of the intriguing historical, archeological and scientific ideas found herein are the subject matter of my other books, especially studies relating to future-past phenomena. Now go forth and *BE* someone.

With Sincerity,

Jason Breshears

About the Author

For more information about Jason Breshears and to explore his work further, please go to www.archaix.com or visit his YouTube channel, Archaix.